TIME TO DANCE

TIME TO DANCE

12 practical dances

FOR THE NON-DANCE SPECIALIST IN
EDUCATION, CHURCH & COMMUNITY

Martin H. Blogg

with Prefaces by Ralph R. Gower,
Anne Hutchinson Guest and Maurice Wood

COLLINS

Collins Liturgical Publications
187 Piccadilly, London W1V 9DA

Collins Liturgical Australia
PO Box 3023 Sydney 2001

ISBN 0 00 599777 1
First published 1984
© 1984 Martin H Blogg

Cover picture:
photo drawing by Steve Store, of the dancer Alison Charles
photo of the author by Tony Saunders
Cover design by Colin Reed
Typographic design by Colin Reed
Typeset by Texet, Leighton Buzzard, Beds
Made and printed by William Collins Sons & Co Ltd, Glasgow

Contents

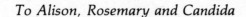

To Alison, Rosemary and Candida

Prefaces

I sat in a gymnasium at the end of a long, hot summer's day to see the Springs Dance Company show teachers how dance could be used to help pupils to understand religion, especially the Christian faith. As one who finds dance difficult to understand anyway, it was not a very welcome prospect! But it was one of those evenings when everything came alive for everyone who was present. After the director of the company, Martin Blogg, explained expression through dance, and demonstrations were given by the company, we entered a new dimension which was potentially rich for religious communication and the evening fled away in the enthusiasm which was generated by the dances and the dancers.

I am therefore delighted to be given the opportunity to write the foreword to Mr. Blogg's book and trust that it will open a new dimension to religious education in Church and in school.

Ralph R. Gower
Staff Inspector for Religious Education
Inner London Education Authority

As editor of the Labanotation of these dances it has given me great pleasure to discover through reading them the enjoyment of the simple movement patterns and the variety in steps and gestures which the dances include. With dance literacy growing, Martin Blogg is indeed looking to the future in including the notation as well as word descriptions. For those already familiar with Labanotation the notated passages facilitate a sight-reading introduction to the material through which the flow and harmony can be immediately revealed.

Ann Hutchinson Guest
Director, The Language of Dance Centre, London

Time to Dance stems from the hard toil of Martin Blogg and his highly professional young dancers and choreographers, working out new patterns of dance and Christian worship.

They have performed in churches, schools and clergy conferences in our diocese, and in our Cathedral and others.

There is plenty of worship today which is sometimes interspersed with ungainly and excited movement. Elsewhere, there is movement of an erotic or frantic sort which is often a substitute for true religion.

Martin Blogg's Springs Dance Company takes Christian worship seriously and sees it in its scriptural perspective, and with disciplined and joyful precision illuminates that worship by truly 'dancing before the Lord'.

Maurice Norvic
Bishop's House, Norwich

Introduction

My concern in this publication is to share, in as simple a form as possible, a basic dance vocabulary, together with a series of uncomplicated dance structures, expressive forms and scriptural ideas within which the untrained dancer may work. Through this non-verbal 'language' I hope some may grow to express something of the heart-felt, ineffable and mystical knowledge and understanding of the Christian faith and worship. I have included in this book a wide variety of dance expressions, ranging from uninhibited physical exuberance in such dances as 'Ding Dong Merrily On High' (8) and 'In The Presence of His People' (4) to the more deeply felt mystical and spiritual expression of 'Salvator Mundi' (3).

Each of the dances tends to focus on one or two particular scriptural and choreographic ideas: a dance structure, an expressive form, or a particular movement pattern. Sometimes the emphasis in the dance is on the steps, at other times on 'dynamics' or expressive energy levels. 'Body shape', 'floor pattern' or 'space pattern' may constitute the primary focus. There is a wide range of simple choreographic possibilities in these dances. Although they are complete in themselves, I hope the dances will not be taken simply in isolation. It is hoped that from a patient practical and theoretical working-out of the various ideas, users of this book will begin to build up a rich vocabulary of possibilities. It is hoped also that from working within these simple structures and ideas they will begin to gain confidence in identifying their own ideas.

SUGGESTIONS ON HOW TO USE THIS BOOK

1. *Firstly*, get an overall feel for the musical accompaniment of the dance:

Time and tempo indicate the rhythmic character of the dance. Time (eg. 2/4, 3/4, 6/8) will make clear the basic rhythmic shape. Tempo (= 116) will indicate the speed of the dance.

Melody will give a clear idea as to the phrase structure and general shape of the composition, significant pauses, climaxes and the beginnings of an emotional feel for the composition.

Harmony will give you a good idea as to the emotional expression of the composition and will reinforce what has been absorbed from the other elements.

Really work on the music before beginning the dance: this will be a great help in realising the movement.

2. *Secondly*, get a good general overview of the dance by identifying the main structures marked $\boxed{A}$, $\boxed{B}$ etc. These, together with the bar markings, correspond to the markings written in the music which precedes each dance.

To translate written instructions into physical movement requires considerable patience, so take this into account and work slowly and carefully. Work with one section at a time and get a good physical grasp of that before moving on to the next. When you think you have grasped the dance sequence, then relate it to the music, by actually physically performing it, keeping to the time, tempo, rhythm, melody and harmony of the piece.

Repeat the dance patterns and physical events over and over again, in order to encourage an internalisation of these physical expressions. You will find that it is some time before the physical events become dance and you are comfortable working with them. Margot Fonteyn says in her biography that she learns the steps quickly but it is a long time before she dances them. So it will be for you. Remember particularly that at least within the context of worship these steps have little or no meaning in themselves. The meaning of the dance lies in what each of us invests in the dance — those physical patterns and sequences described in words. And fundamental to this is scripture. Each dance described here has its roots in scripture and it is important to study the text carefully.

Which brings us to the *third* focus.

3. Having attained a good knowledge and understanding of the music and the dance events, now consider carefully the drama or meaning of the text. Each dance has a different meaning. It is important to identify and articulate that meaning if you are to begin to bring the dance alive, taking it beyond a mere physical sequence of events. The same problem faces the actor who has to make the words come alive and the musician who has to invest something of himself in the notes as described in musical notation. Although most of the dances are based upon a verbal text, each dance is not principally a literal or mimetic expression: it is not intended to convey a narrative but rather the inner meaning and deeper understanding of the text.

4. *Fourthly*, the dancers should concentrate now on accuracy and precision in the dance, both individually and collectively. Give attention to moving together, stepping accurately in both space and physical terms. The space or geometric element of choreography is a major element in these dances. With geometry in mind, give careful attention to line in the body ... where should the head be, where should the arms be, the R shoulder etc. Think about the sound, the costume, the drama, the setting ... all those elements that go to make up a performance. Yes, I use this term quite deliberately for what you are after IS a performance in the sense of a skilful, disciplined presentation aimed at in some sense communicating the Christian faith. The performance I hasten to add is not an end in itself, as it is in the theatre. The performance is a *means* to worship.

A FEW WORDS ABOUT THE RELATIONSHIP BETWEEN SINGING AND DANCING

First, let me say that all these songs can be sung and danced at the same time. Indeed, they were originally conceived to be performed in this way, since it is sometimes difficult to get hold of suitable recordings, or to rely on a group of singers who have the necessary sympathy and understanding as well as the expertise to accompany the dances.

However I do recognise that singing and dancing at the same time might present a problem for those who have enough difficulty coping with the steps of the dances, without adding singing as well; and that some of the more energetic dances demand more 'puff' than is comfortable if one is also to sing during worship.

So there is no compulsion either way in this relationship. Having an independent vocal and/or instrumental group — either recorded or 'live' — is as valid as having all the dancers sing and dance at the same time. Where it is possible to choose between the two methods, I do feel that there are some dances where to have the vocal accompaniment performed by the dancers themselves would greatly enhance the worship. For example:

Father, we adore you
Salvator mundi
Make me an instrument
Gloria

An independent instrumental/vocal group might be more appropriate with such lively and energetic dances as

Sing unto our Father
In the presence of your people

God has spoken
Ding dong merrily on high

Those dances which rely on a carefully developed and interesting accompaniment to keep the repetition alive, or to provide sympathetic support for expressions with a less literal focus, might benefit from an independent accompaniment, e.g.:

Adoramus to Domine
Quem pastores
Infant holy

(see also what I have said about the musical accompaniment after Adoremus te Domine, no.10 below).

Some notes on the *Placing of Dances* will be found after Salvator Mundi, no.3 below.

A FEW WORDS ABOUT COSTUME FOR THE CHURCH DANCE CHOIR

Allow freedom of movement. Make sure that the form of the costume, the texture of the material, its hang and its flow allow sufficient freedom to move.

Do not have a costume that gives so much freedom that the body, which after all is the primary vehicle for expression, can no longer be seen. Remember that body shape and line constitute, in part at least, the raw material of dance. Consider how the costume can enhance this aspect of expression.

Consider modesty and decency within the context of your own fellowship. Above all, take considerable thought and care before using leotards and tights. My experience is that this costume has been a bigger stumbling block in the acceptance of dance in worship than any other factor. Whilst it is a normal and legitimate costume for dance rehearsals and for the theatrical dance world, it may not be the right costume for dance in worship.

Aim for classical simplicity of line and colour, to allow the beauty and skill of the body to be presented at its best. Do not go in for fussy extras. Get rid of jewellery, rings, watches, ribbons etc. Above all, never let the costume upstage the worship of the dance. All too often I have seen spectacular costumes which have become ends in themselves. They may be aesthetically attractive and skilfully made, but should not become more important than the worship, and the dance which is a means to worship.

Remember that the costume is an intimate part of the dance expression for worship and not simply a covering of the body. Think carefully about a pattern that will be flexible and versatile in both artistic and dancers' terms. Think of the colour, texture, hang and form of the material. Think about the fact that your dancers will come in all sorts of shapes and sizes, and that these 'all sorts' will change as time goes on. The form that is eventually decided on should be the one that is the most flattering for the group and one that is easily adjusted.

With these principles in mind, and speaking from my own experience, I would suggest the following:

A good, not too expensive material is jersey crepe. It hangs well and does not crease easily. It washes well. It is easy to cut and does not need a hem. It has sufficient stretch to allow a snug fitting. There is usually a good variety of colours available. With regard to colour, I would suggest a monochrome approach: for example, various shades of purple, pink, mauve and blue. This gives interest and allows versatility.

A carefully tailored bodice, with long sleeves, fitting snugly, is good. 'A 'V' neck and full skirt, ankle length, with at least a complete circle at the hem line gives tremendous scope for dance. The whole dress could be made in vertical panels, rather than with a separate bodice and skirt. I have found this vertical line is far the most flattering for dancers; it hangs and flows much better than the separate bodice and skirt, and above all, it is much easier to alter.

Costume for men

All that has been said with regard to women's costume applies in general terms to men's. A simple but well-tailored open-neck shirt with long sleeves fitting at the wrist, and a well-fitting pair of trousers which emphasise the line of the legs are needed. The trousers should be made of a stretch material, to allow freedom of movement and a good fit.

Note

In what I have said about costume, I have had in mind a regular, specialist church dance choir. Of course, if the dances are used with members of the congregation — and there is no reason why those given in this book should not be — then the whole question of costume becomes relatively unimportant, though it might be wise to recommend that people wear clothing which allows freedom of movement.

A FEW WORDS ABOUT LABANOTATION

Let me say first of all that it is not essential to have a knowledge of this recording system in order to realise the dances in this book. The method of recording dance ideas in words is quite efficient and effective without the notation. I have included the Labanotation as an Appendix, for the following reasons:

1. It has to be said that to describe dance in words is limited, and capable only of giving simple and general ideas of movement. To write down all the potential movement possibilities in words would be extremely cumbersome and in the end would undermine the task of communication. In the Labanotation given in the Appendix, it has been possible to give much more detail about the dances than words alone can convey. For the notator, then, this method offers a refined, a more subtle and detailed picture of physical possibilities.

2. In recent years there has been an extraordinary development in the field of dance notation as a recording system for all sorts of dance within theatre, ethnic dance, social dance, dance therapy. In professional dance companies the dance notator is now a norm. When a new dance is being created, the dance notator carefully records every movement. When a work from the repertoire is reproduced, once again the notator is there to advise on what was actually danced. Dance notation, then, is a normal part of dance and it is right that these dances should be written in this way.

3. The recognition of dance notation as a legitimate and normal part of the dance world is reflected in the recent London University 'O' and 'A' level dance examinations. The ISTD have recently recorded all the National Dance Syllabus. The Royal Academy of Dance has recorded much of the Ballet Grade Syllabus. Dance notation constitutes a proper field of study within the education of a dancer. Since this book is aimed at schools as well as the community and the church it is hoped that the RE department and the Dance department will work together to realise some of this material.

MARTIN H. BLOGG

A cassette recording of the music for these dances is available from the publisher.

1 Father We Adore You

A beautiful meditative three-part canon
for a large number of dancers

Terrye Coelho

1. Fa - ther)
2. Je - sus } we a - dore you; lay our lives be - fore you. How we love you.
3. Spi - rit)

Music	Bar	Beat	Movement
4/4 ♩=76			**Starting position** Dancers make three circles, as in the diagram. Stand tall with feet together, facing the centre of the circles. Arms are held loosely across the chest with wrists crossed right in front of left. The palms are open. The head is tilted forwards.
A	1		*'Father we a-...* Slowly let the head come up to focus forward 'high' on an imaginary cross. At the same time let both arms come outstretched before you with the wrists still crossed. Palms are open and face upwards.
	2		*'...dore you'* Let the arms open out wide to the side and then wide and high above the head in adoration. Palms remain open and facing up.
B	3/4		*'Lay our lives before you'* Step back with the R/f and slowly come to kneel on the R knee with the arms held out wide in front. The head is tilted slightly forwards. The whole is an attitude of supplication.
C	5/6		*'How we love you'* The head comes up, once again focusing on the imaginary cross forwards 'high'. The body comes to stand, expressing an attitude of peace, wonder, love and praise.
			In these three motifs we have the basic movement vocabulary which each of the three circle groups perform in canon, commencing with the inner circle and working outwards. I suggest that the canon is performed three times, corresponding to the three verses of the song. When the inner circles have completed the three verses, they come to stand still and quiet until the other circles finish.

EXTENDED VERSION OF 'FATHER WE ADORE YOU'

Section One

All those taking part in the dance quietly and carefully move into their set positions in the three circles. Remember that *how* people get into position is an important part of the dance and should reflect something of the spiritual atmosphere and drama of the dance meditation. When you come to your position kneel in as comfortable a position as possible, ideally sitting back on the feet. Arms are held loosely across the chest and the head is tilted slightly forward.

In this position all 'hum' the melody *three* times in canon. The humming is intended to evoke the appropriate spiritual atmosphere before the movement.

Give some thought to the arrangement of these three circles: e.g. the centre circle could consist of the children, the second of women and the third of men. This arrangement allows three different voice colours and also encourages an increase or build-up of sound.

Consider also the visual aspect of the circles' composition: for example, the height of the dancers, the placing of men and women, and so on.

Section Two

When each circle group has completed the humming they very carefully, in time together, bring the L/f forward and rise into the position of the dance. They now perform the singing and movement already described. Remember that each circle will do this at a different time. When the inner circle rises and goes into the singing the other two will still be humming. Do practise the getting up, for this can be very untidy!

Try to develop a continuing build-up of sound in volume, strength and confidence.

I suggest that this is performed three times, to correspond to the three verses of the song.

Section Three

On the completion of the three song/movements, each group gives the peace. The first group, because it finishes Section Two first, will begin by giving the peace to the other members of the inner circle. But as soon as possible they move into the second and third circles. Similarly as soon as the second and third circles finish their action/singing, they move into the other circles and greet each other with the peace. Everyone continues singing his or her part in the canon. This is important in keeping the atmosphere of the dance and singing alive. How the greeting in the peace is given does not matter as long as all keep singing accurately and confidently.

During this section, consider inviting the rest of the fellowship to take a part in the peace, either by encouraging them to come and join the dancers where they are, or by each of the three circles of dancers going out into the congregation and giving the peace.

Throughout the whole dance, the congregation should be encouraged to take a part in the humming and singing. This dance event should be primarily participatory.

To bring the dance meditation to an end, the leader gives a sign, and eventually all the dancers, wherever they are, turn to face the cross and complete their verse for the last time. It is very effective if silence is kept for a few moments, and possibly the leader of the fellowship could end with a short prayer.

2 Sing to our Father

A joyful, vigorous and uninhibited dance
based upon simple folk dance motifs.

Stephen Ball
Jon Wilkes

Lorna Ball

1. Sing to our Fa - ther, Cre - a - tor and King, who sent his Son, Je - sus, to
2. Sing to our broth-er, who of him-self poured out life to his peo-ple to
3. Sing to the Spi - rit, _ let us all hear and know that he frees us from

suf - fer and bring us in - to his fam' - ly. Oh, mag - ni - fy him!
see them re - stored. _ Sing to our heal - er and sing to our Lord!
sin and from fear to love one an - oth - er, to serve and to care.

Sing, sing, sing, sing, sing to the Lord of { love! / life! / peace!

Al - le - lu - ia, al - le - lu - ia,

al - le - lu - ia, al - le - lu - ia! Clap! Clap!

Music	Bar	Beat	Movement
6/8 ♩=116	◯		**Starting position** The dancers stand to face the centre of a circle ready to side skip to the L. Dancers join hands with those on either side, and arms are held low. Dancers are identified as A and B alternately.

Music	Bar	Beat	Movement
A	1	1 & 2 &	Step L/f to L. Close R/f to L with weight on R/f. Step L/f to L. Close R/f to L with weight on R/f. } 3 skips and a hop to L
	2	1 & 2 &	Step L/f to L. Close R/f to L with weight on R/f. Step L/f to L. Hop on L/f.
	3	1 & 2 &	Step R/f to R. Close L/f to L with weight on L/f. Step R/f to R. Close L/f to L with weight on L/f. } 3 skips and a hop to R
	4	1 & 2 &	Step R/f to R. Close L/f to L with weight on L/f. Step R/f to R. Hop R/f.
	5	1 & 2 &	Step L/f to L. Close R/f to L with weight on R/f. Step L/f to L. Hop on L/f. } L
	6	1 & 2 &	Step R/f to R. Close L/f to R with weight on L/f. Step R/f to R. Hop on R/f. } R
	7	1 & 2 &	Step L/f to L. Hop on L/f. Step R/f to R. Hop on R. } Let go of partners' hands. Bring arms high and wide above the head in an uninhibited expression of praise.
	8	1 & 2 &	Step L/f to L. Hop on L/f. Step R/f to R. Hop on R.
	9	1 & 2 &	Step L/f to L. Close R/f to L with weight on R/f. Step L/f to L. Close R/f to L with weight on R/f. } circle L
	10	1 & 2 &	Step L/f to L. Close R/f to L with weight on R/f. Step L/f to L. Hop on L/f.

During bars 9 and 10 complete a small individual circle to the L and come to face the centre of the circle. Lower the arms.

Music	Bar	Beat	Movement		
			A Group	**B Group**	
B	11	1 2	Step R/f forward Step L/f forward	Step R/f forward Step L/f forward	1 small individual circle to the R.
	12	2 2	Step R/f forward Bring L/f to R but keep weight on R.	Step R/f forward Step L/f forward	
			During these three steps A's come into the circle centre, bending the trunk forward low as they do so and arriving with trunk 'high'. At the same time they bring their arms firstly across the body and then up to the side, high and wide above the head.		
	13	1 2	Step L/f back Step R/f back	Pivot turning to the R on the R/f with arms high and wide above the head.	
	14	1 2	Step L/f back Bring R/f to L but keep weight on L.		
			During these steps A's retreat from the centre. Arms remain high and wide above the head and the trunk is held slightly leaning back with head focused forward high.		
			Arms of both A and B come down at the end of this motif.		
	15/18		*Repeat Bars 11-14*, but A's perform B's motif B's perform A's motif		

(Note: "Forward" brace spans bars 11-12 A Group; "Backward" brace spans bars 13-14 A Group.)

Music	Bar	Beat	Movement
Repeat $\boxed{B^2}$			**Variation during the repeat**
			The last eight bars of music (i.e. bars 11-18) are repeated but this time instead of A's and B's performing different motifs both perform together the original sequence of group A.
	11	1 2	Step R/f forward Step L/f forward
	12	1 2	Step R/f forward Bring L/f to R but keep weight on R
			During these three steps ALL come into the centre bending trunk forward low as they do so and arriving with trunk 'high'. At the same time they bring their arms across the body and then out to the side and high then wide above the head.
	13	1 2	Step L/f back Step R/f back
	14	1 2	Step L/f back Bring R/f to L but keep weight on L
			During these steps ALL retreat from the centre. Arms remain high and wide above the head and the trunk is slightly leaned back with the head focused high.
			Arms come down at the end of this motif.
	15	1 2	Step R/f forward Step L/f forward
	16	1 2	Step R/f forward Step L/f forward
	17/18		Pivot turning to the R on the R/f with arms high and wide above the head.
			Hold still this position, facing centre for clapping.
	19	1 2	Clap! Clap!
			Note: on the completion of the two claps the arms come down and return to the beginning position, hands clasped with neighbours.

Bracket annotations: bars 11–12 — "forward"; bars 13–14 — "backward"; bars 15–16 — "a small individual circle away from the circle to the R."

3 Salvator Mundi

'SAVIOUR OF THE WORLD, SAVE US, FREE US'

A simple but deeply moving spiritual meditation
in movement

Music	Bar	Beat	Movement
4/4 ♩ = 80			**Starting position** All kneel sitting back on the heels. Arms are held loosely across the chest with the wrists crossed R in front of L but not touching. The palms of the hand are open and facing the body. The head is tilted forward slightly. **See separate diagram for 'placing' possibilities (p.18).**
			Instrumental Introduction It is in the instrumental introduction that the spiritual mood is set for both dancers and congregation.
A	1-2	1-8	To the count of 8, i.e. 2 bars, slowly lift the head up forward high to focus on the cross.
B	3	1-4	To the count of 4 rise up 'high' on the knees letting the upper torso lean back. At the same time the arms come outstretched to the front with wrists crossed and palms facing upwards in an attitude of supplication.
	4	1-4	Bring the body upright and let the arms open out wide to the side, slightly diagonally forward. The hands remain palms uppermost. At the same time the L/leg comes forward in preparation for getting up. Try to do this in such a way that the focus remains on the upper half of the body, so that the movement of the leg is hardly noticed.

Music	Bar	Beat	Movement
C	5	1-4	Come to stand tall with feet together, by bringing the weight of the body to the extended L/leg. Keep the face focused high on the cross and let the arms come down to the sides. On the 4th beat, rise up on the balls of the feet.
	6	1-4	Keep the face focused on the cross and leading with the R shoulder walk 'high' four steps to the R and come to face the cross again.
D	7	1-4	Step back with the R leg to kneel 'high' on that knee. Take the full four beats to go slowly down.
	8	1-4	Slowly and carefully return to the original position of bar 1. The head is tilted forwards once again and the arms with wrists crossed are placed across the chest.

The whole is repeated as many times as required.

POSSIBILITIES FOR DEVELOPING THIS VERY SIMPLE IDEA

There are a number of things that can be done with this very simple movement sequence.

The simplest and most obvious is to have every dancer doing exactly the same, in unison. This is probably the best way for all to become familiar with the movement sequence.

But consider the following:

Idea One

1. Solo dancer performs the movement sequence.

2. Solo dancer is joined by *three more* dancers and the movement sequence is performed by these four together.

3. Solo dancer, plus these three, plus *five more* dancers, making a total of nine dancers, perform the movement sequence together.

The diagram shows a suggested 'placing' for these three stages.

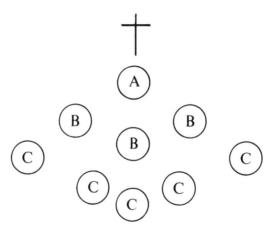

Idea Two   Now, consider Idea One in terms of a movement canon. Divide into four groups, to match the four parts of the music. Each group begins the movement sequence in turn, performing the sequence for an agreed number of times and finishing in turn.

This may be done within the placing already suggested for Idea One, with the addition of group D.

Idea Three   Consider the various 'placing' possibilities for the four groups either in unison or in canon. These can either be complete four part canon groups in themselves or the four parts can be placed to face in different directions: for example, group one might all face L diagonally forward, while group two might be placed to face in the opposite direction. See below for 'placing' ideas.

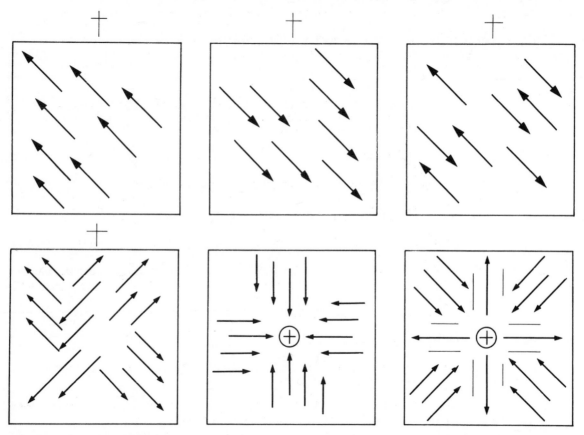

'Placing', i.e. the position in space where the dancer(s) are set, is a much neglected and underestimated choreographic focus. Some very interesting effects can be obtained by considering not the movement so much as the actual placing of the dancers. Experiment with some of the ideas I have suggested, and with other combinations. Think up your own ideas about spacing. Consider *how* the dancers actually get into their places. Will they be placed before the dance begins, or will they move into their places, incorporating this movement into the dance expression?

A consideration that runs through this practical dance book is that meaning does not lie in the movement itself, but rather in what each dancer brings to the movement. With this in mind, consider using the movement ideas we have just given for *Salvator mundi* for a very different spiritual expression. I have in mind the *Benedictus* from the Taizé music (*Music from Taizé*, vocal edition, p.88).

From 'Saviour of the world, save us, free us' we move to 'Blessed is he who comes in the name of the Lord'. Whilst the movements remain basically the same in physical terms, the text, the music and the individual expression with which we invest the movements will bring about an altogether different dance composition.

4 In the Presence of Your People

A lively and joyful community dance
based upon simple folk dance motifs

Psalm 22:3,25   Brent Chambers

In the pres-ence of your peo-ple I will praise your name,

for a-lone you are ho-ly, en-throned on the prais-es of Is-ra-el.

Let us cel-e-brate your good-ness and your stead-fast love.

May your name be ex-alt-ed here on earth and in heav'n a-bove.

Music	Bar	Beat	Movement
4/4 ♩=116	◯		**Starting position** Dancers, identified as A and B, form a circle and face the centre. Each dancer clasps the hand of the person on either side. Arms are held low

Music	Bar	Beat	Movement
A	1	1 & 2 & 3 & 4 &	**Main theme** Step R/f forward. ⎫ Bend R knee. ⎪ Step L/f forward. ⎬ face R and travel Bend L knee. ⎪ anti-clockwise Step R/f forward. ⎪ Bend R knee. ⎪ Step L/f forward. ⎭ Bend L knee and turn to face centre. The term 'bend' indicates a giving in the knee which produces a lively bouncy effect.
	2	1 & 2 3 & 4	{ Step R/f to R side. Keep weight on R/f. { Bend R knee. (Stamp L/f alongside R/f. { Step L/f to L side. Keep weight on L/f. { Bend L knee. (Stamp R/f alongside L/f.
B	3	1 & 2 & 3 & 4 &	Step R/f to R side. Bend R knee. Step L/f 'deep' behind R/f. Bend L knee. Step R/f 'high' to R side. Bend R knee. Step L/f in front of R/f to R side. Bend L knee.
	4	1 & 2 3 & 4	{ Step R/f to R side. Keep weight on R/f. { Bend R knee. (Stamp L/f alongside R/f. Release hands. Stamp L/f. Clap hands above head! Stamp R/f. Clap hands above head! Stamp L/f. Clap hands above head!

(Brace spanning bars 2–4: face into centre of circle)

Music	Bar	Beat	Movement	
			A's	**B's**
C	5	1 & 2 & 3 & 4 &	Step R/f forward. Bend R knee. Step L/f forward. Bend L knee. Step R/f forward. Bend R knee. Step L/f forward Bend L knee. } forward As dancers enter the centre of the circle, bend the trunk forward moving from 'deep' to 'high' with the arms crossing the chest, with R arm over L arm, to open out high and wide above the head in praise.	Step R/f to R. Bend R knee. Step L/f forward. Bend L knee. Step R/f forward. Bend R knee. Step L/f forward. Bend L knee. } circle to R Keep the arms above the head in praise. Walk a small individual circle moving away from the main circle to these four steps.
	6	1 & 2 & 3 & 4 &	Step R/f back. Bend R knee. Step L/f back. Bend L knee. Step R/f back. Bend R knee. Step L/f back. Bend L knee. } backwards Keep the arms high and wide above the head as you step back and let the upper torso lean back with the head looking high forward.	'Pivot turn' on the R/f to R. ending facing centre of circle. Bring the arms down on the completion of the pivot turn.
D	7	1 & 2 & 3 & 4 &	Step R/f to R. Bend R knee. Step L/f forward. Bend L knee. Step R/f forward. Bend R knee. Step L/f forward. Bend L knee. } circle to R Keep arms high and wide above the head in praise. Form a small individual circle moving away and out of the main circle to these four steps.	Step R/f forward. Bend R knee. Step L/f forward. Bend L knee. Step R/f forward. Bend R knee. Step L/f forward. Bend L knee. } forward As dancers enter the centre of the circle, bend the trunk forward moving from 'deep' to 'high' with the arms crossing the chest, with R arm over L arm, to open out wide and high above the head in praise.

Music	Bar	Beat	Movement	
			A's	**B's**
	8	1 & 2 & 3 & 4 &	'Pivot Turn' on the R/f to the R. End facing centre of circle.	Step R/f back. Bend R knee. Step L/f back. Bend L knee. Step R/f back. ⎫ Bend R knee. ⎬ backward Step L/f back. ⎭ Bend L knee.
			On the completion of the pivot turn, bring the arms down, ready to take the hand of partners and commence the dance from the beginning.	Dancers keep the arms high and wide above the head as they step backwards and let the torso lean back with the head held high forward. Bring the arms down on the fourth step back, ready to commence the whole dance from the beginning. Take the hands of partners.

Repeat from beginning   Ideally, the song is sung many times and each repeat brings a gradual increase in tempo.

EXTENDED VERSION

Main Theme   The dance as already notated — the full eight bars, with congregation and dancers singing.

Variation One   Whilst the singers continue with the song the dancers perform the ancient folk dance motif *'The Hey'*. Dancers already identified as A and B turn to face each other in opposite directions. A's turn to the R and B's turn to the left. Everyone is now facing a partner and ready to move off in the direction they are facing. Both step off with the R/f giving R hands to R hands and passing R shoulder to R shoulder. Take two steps between each greeting. The second greeting is done by giving L hand to L hand and passing L shoulder to L shoulder and so on alternately. Make 14 changes in all, and for the remaining beats of the music, walk an individual circle on the spot, in order to get back into a comfortable starting position and take the hands of your partners once again.

     This 'hey' represents 'the peace' and is a genuine greeting of each other.

     This second rendering of the song might be an instrumental one, to give a sense of varied instrumental colour.

Main Theme   Return to the original dance as notated i.e. Main Theme.

Variation Two   *Farandole.* This is essentially follow the leader. One of the dancers leads everyone in the form of a snake or chain producing a variety of floor patterns, perhaps down the aisle of the church.

     This is best done with an instrumental backing, since it is sometimes difficult to judge the music for getting back to original performance position.

Main Theme   Finally a return to the original dance with everyone singing and instrumentalists giving their all in a dramatic and joyful conclusion. Finish cleanly if you possibly can, with absolute stillness and silence. Whatever happens, do not let the dance come to an untidy finish.

5 Prayer of St Francis

A simple meditative dance

S. Temple, 1967   S. Temple, 1967

1. Make me a chan-nel of your peace. _____ Where
2. Make me a chan-nel of your peace. _____ Where

there is ha-tred, let me bring your love. _____ Where
there's de-spair in life, let me bring hope. _____ Where

there is in-ju-ry, your par-don, Lord. _____ And
there is dark-ness _____ on-ly light, _____ And

where there's doubt, true faith in _____ you. _____
where there's sad-ness ev - er _____ joy. _____

Refrain

Oh, Mas-ter, grant that I may nev-er seek _____ So

much to be con-soled as to con-sole. _____ To be

un-der-stood as to un-der-stand. _____ To be

loved, as to love, with all my soul. _____

Verse 3   Make me a channel of your peace.
It is in pardoning that we are pardoned,
in giving to all men that we receive;
and in dying that we're born to eternal life.   *Refrain*

Music	Bar	Beat	Movement
2/4 ♩=**84**			**Starting position** All kneel low, sitting back on the feet, in a circle facing the centre. The arms are held loosely across the chest with wrists crossed right in front of left but not touching. The palms of the hands are open and face inwards towards the body. The head is tilted slightly forward. The whole suggests an attitude of prayer and contemplation. Dancers identified as A and B alternately.
A	1-4		**Motif One** *'Make me a channel of your peace'.* Slowly the head is raised and the face comes to focus on the cross forwards/high. At the same time the arms reach forward with palms open facing upwards in an attitude of petition. Wrists remain crossed. There is a physical and emotional quietness, a reverence and humility implicit in these simple movements as we offer ourselves to his service i.e. 'to be made a channel of *his* peace'.
B	5-8		**Motif Two** From the outstretched petitioning position of the first motif the arms now open wide to the side and slightly diagonally forward, just below the horizontal. Hands are open with palms facing upwards. At the same time slowly rise up on to the knees. If possible, keep the body weight tilted back, the head in line with the back and the arms stretching away to the front. The attitude here is of opening our whole being — not just our arms — to *his* service and asking the Lord to come into our hearts, our minds and our bodies in order that we may truly be effective in bringing 'consolation', 'hope' and 'pardon'.
C	9-12		**Motif Three** From the previous kneeling high position bring the L leg carefully forward in preparation for getting up into a standing position. Remain kneeling on the R knee. At the same time the torso now leans forward with arms outstretched low and diagonally behind the body. The head is tilted slightly forward. Here the attitude is one of humility, a recognition of our unworthiness and utter weakness and the impossibility of our being able to do anything without his love, his strength, his grace and mercy. We are utterly dependent upon him.

Music	Bar	Beat	Movement
D	13-16		**Motif Four** Bring the weight of the body forward onto the R leg. Carefully come to stand tall and confident strong in the Lord with the head held high in the full assurance of faith that his love will work within each of us.
Refrain	17-32		The movement meditation up to now has been essentially personal based upon what is sometimes referred to as 'the vertical relationship' with our Lord. The 'vertical relationship' is now translated into everyday life and expressed in 'horizontal' terms i.e. between each other. This is symbolised and acted out in the form of the English folk dance motif 'the hey'. **The Hey** All A's turn to the right and all B's turn to the left, so that each faces a partner. Both move off at the same time in opposite directions from the facing each other position. Both start with the R/f passing R shoulder to R shoulder giving R hands in greeting. They then pass on to the next person L shoulder to L shoulder giving L hands and so on alternately. This corresponds to the 'peace' in church fellowship. Slowly and very sensitively move among each other travelling in opposite directions taking each other's hand(s) and reminding each other that God's 'peace', 'love', 'hope', 'light', 'joy', 'pardon', and 'understanding' — all expressions from the text of St Francis's prayer — have to be realised through one another. The 'peace' may be performed freely in relation to the music with the singing acting as an impressionistic background to the movement. Dancers might feel that trying to keep in strict time with this refrain will make the expression rather stilted and false. However it is possible to move in time, and I suggest that *six* changes of direction are made, with four small steps between each change, or three small steps and a pause. For the few remaining beats of the music after the six changes, each dancer walks quietly and carefully on the spot in preparation for kneeling down once again, ready to return to the original prayer position of the beginning.

Repeat from the beginning

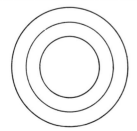

It may be that there are too many people wanting to take part in this very popular and simple dance meditation for one circle. If so, form two or three circles on the outside of the original one. See diagram.

6 God Has Spoken

A strong, dramatic community dance based upon simple Israeli folk dance steps expressing with uninhibited urgency the fundamental importance of listening to God's word

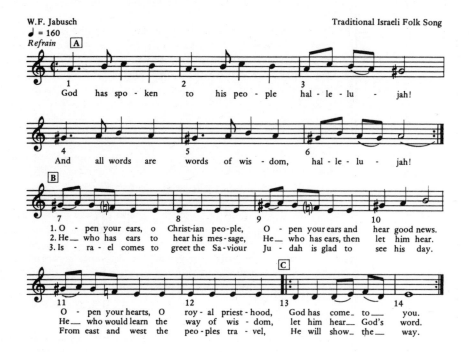

W.F. Jabusch

Traditional Israeli Folk Song

♩ = 160

Refrain

A

1 God has spo-ken   2 to his peo-ple   3 hal-le-lu-jah!

4 And all words are   5 words of wis-dom,   6 hal-le-lu-jah!

B

7 1. O - pen your ears, o   8 Christ-ian peo-ple,   9 O - pen your ears and   10 hear good news.
2. He— who has ears to   hear his mes-sage,   He— who has ears, then   let him hear.
3. Is - ra - el comes to   greet the Sa-viour   Ju - dah is glad to   see his day.

11 O - pen your hearts, O   12 roy - al priest-hood,   13 God has come to— **C** 14 you.
He— who would learn the   way of wis-dom,   let him hear— God's word.
From east and west the   peo-ples tra - vel,   He will show— the— way.

Music	Bar	Beat	Movement
4/4 ♩=160	◯		**Starting position** Dancers stand in a circle clasping the hands of the person on either side. Arms are held at shoulder level.

Music	Bar	Beat	Movement
A	1	1	Step L/f 'deep' behind R/f ... accent!
		2	Step R/f 'high' side R.
		3	Step L/f 'medium' R diagonal/forward.
		4	Step R/f 'medium' R side.
	2	1	Step L/f 'deep' behind R/f ... accent!
		2	Step R/f 'high' side R.
		3	Step L/f 'medium' R diagonal/forward.
		4	Hop on L/f. } Travel R. Face centre of circle.
	3	1	Step R/f forward. } small individual
		2	Step L/f forward. circular path on
		3	Step R/f forward. the spot ... to the
		4	Hop on R/f. *left.*
			Note: release hands on turn. Take partners' hands again for bar 4.
	4	1	Step L/f 'deep' behind R/f ... accent!
		2	Step R/f 'high' side R.
		3	Step L/f 'medium' R diagonal/forward.
		4	Step R/f 'medium' R side.
	5	1	Step L/f 'deep' behind R/f ... accent!
		2	Step R/f 'high' side R.
		3	Step L/f 'medium' R diagonal/forward.
		4	Hop on L/f. } Travel R. Face centre of circle.
	6	1	Step R/f forward. } small individual
		2	Step L/f forward. circular path on
		3	Step R/f forward. the spot ... to the
		4	Hop on R/f. *Left.*
			Note: release hands on turn.
			Repeat bars 1-6 as in music.
B	7	1	Step L/f back.
		2	Hop on L/f. } Arms come individually
		3	Step R/f back. diagonally forwards 'high'.
		4	Hop on R/f.
	8	1	Stamp L/f forward 'deep'.
		2	Stamp R/f forward 'deep'. } Arms come down to the side and fists
		3	Stamp L/f forward 'deep'. are clenched.
		4	Stamp R/f forward 'deep'.

Music	Bar	Beat	Movement
	9	1 2 3 4	Step L/f back. Hop on L/f. } Arms come individually Step R/f back. } diagonally forwards 'high'. Hop on R/f.

	10	1
		2
		
		3
		4
			Step L/f diagonally forward L.
			Brush the R/f through and extend } Arms open
			  it to the L/D. } diagonally forwards
			Step R/f diagonally forward R. } 'medium'.
			Brush the L/f through and extend
			  it to the L/D.

	11	1 2 3 4	Step L/f back. Hop on L/f. } Arms come individually Step R/f back. } diagonally forwards 'high'. Hop on R/f.
	12	1 2 3 4	Stamp L/f forwards 'deep'. } Arms come down to Stamp R/f forwards 'deep'. } the side and fists Stamp L/f forwards 'deep'. } are clenched. Hop on L/f.
C	13	1 2 3 4	Step R/f forwards. } Small circular path to the R Step L/f forwards. } with small running steps. Arms gradually Step R/f forwards. } coming up high and wide above the Step L/f forwards. } head … palms open and facing upwards.
	14	1-4	*'Pivot Turn'* to the R. Arms gradually come down in the pivot|turn.
			Repeat bars 13-14, turning to left.
			Repeat from beginning

Study the words of the text very carefully and invest something of their meaning in the suggested movement. Remember that the movements in themselves are meaningless within the context of worship until each of us invests something of ourselves in it. Note the suggested tempo as well as the emotional and physical energy level of a song like this.

7 Infant Holy, Infant Lowly

A gentle but joyful nativity dance
based upon the 16th century Branle

Tr. Edith M. Reed

Polish carol

1. In - fant ho - ly, In - fant low - ly, For his bed a cat - tle stall;
2. Flocks were sleep - ing, Shep-herds keep - ing Vi - gil till the morn - ing new;
3. Thus re - joic - ing, Free from sor - row, Prai - ses voic - ing, Greet the mor - row,

Ox - en low - ing, Lit - tle know - ing Christ the Babe is Lord of all.
Saw the glo - ry, Heard the sto - ry, Ti - dings of a gos - pel true.
Christ the Babe was born for you! Christ the Babe was born for you!

Refrain

Swift are wing - ing An - gels sing - ing, No-wells ring - ing, Ti - dings bring - ing,

Christ the Babe is Lord of all, Christ the Babe is Lord of all.

Melody © Bell & Hyman.

Music	Bar	Beat	Movement	
3/4 ♩=92	⊕		**Starting position** The dancers stand to face the centre of a circle focusing on an imaginary crib in which the infant Jesus lies. Hands are held at shoulder level with the palms of each hand just touching the palms of the person either side. The head is tilted slightly forward and over, as if looking into the crib. Feet are together.	
A	1	1 2 3	**Verse 1** Step R/f 'high' to R. Bring L/f to R/f — both 'high'. Lower both heels gently to the ground.	During this movement the head turns diagonally forward/R
	2	1 2 3	Step L/f 'high' to L. Bring R/f to L/f — both 'high'. Lower both heels gently to the ground. On the second half of this beat bend the knees slightly in preparation for the joyful motif of the next bar.	During this movement the head turns diagonally forward/L.

Music	Bar	Beat	Movement
	3	1	Step backwards 'high' with R/f and bring the L/f to the R/f on the second half of the beat. At the same time release your partners' hands and let the arms come up high and wide above the head in praise with palms horizontal facing upwards. The head is tilted slightly back with the face forwards 'high'.
		2	Stay 'high' and remain perfectly still.
		3	Lower both heels gently to the ground. On the second half of the beat bend the knees slightly.
	4	1	Step forwards 'high' with L/f and bring the R/f to the L/f on the second half of the beat. The arms retain the position of the previous bar but the head this time tilts slightly forward looking down at the infant Jesus.
		2	Stay 'high' and remain perfectly still.
		3	Lower both heels gently to the ground and return to original hand contact position.
B	5	1 2 3	Step L/f 'high' to L. Bring R/f to L/f — both 'high'. Lower both heels gently to the ground.
	6	1 2 3	Step R/f 'high' to R. Bring L/f to R/f — both 'high'. Lower both heels gently to the ground. On the second half of the beat bend the knees slightly in preparation for a new motif bars 7/8. Head as for bars 1 and 2.
	7	1 2 3	Step L/f 'high'. Step R/f 'high'. Step L/f 'high'.
	8	1 2 3	Step R/f 'high'. Step L/f 'high'. Step R/f 'high'

With these six steps to the L in an anti-clockwise direction, tread an individual 1¼ circle. Finish facing to the L, ready for the Refrain.

During bars 7 and 8, these six walks 'high', where possible keep the focus on the infant all the time. This produces a lovely effect from the shoulders. During these walks, the arms come slowly down to the side, so that the hands of the partner on each side are again taken, this time held low.

Music	Bar	Beat	Movement
C	9	1 2 3	**Refrain:** facing clockwise and travelling in the same direction. Step L/f forward 'deep'. ⎱ Torso leans towards the L. Let Step R/f forward 'high'. ⎬ the head look over the L shoulder. Step L/f forward 'high'. ⎰ Both ideas taking the three beats.
	10	1 2 3	Step R/f forward 'deep'. ⎱ Torso leans towards the R. Let Step L/f forward 'high'. ⎬ the head look over the R shoulder. Step R/f forward 'high'. ⎰ Both ideas taking the three beats.
	11	1 2 3	Step L/f forward 'deep'. ⎱ Torso leans towards the L. Let Step R/f forward 'high'. ⎬ the head look over the L shoulder. Step L/f forward high'. ⎰ Both ideas taking the three beats. During bars 9-11 of the refrain the arms, to a count of nine beats, are slowly brought up high above the head in a growing expression of joy and wonder. The L arm comes forwards 'high' and the R arm comes backwards 'high'. Partners' hands remain in contact until the climax of this expressive motif — the 'pivot turn' — when hands are released with palms facing upwards and horizontal.
	12	1 & 2 & 3 &	Turn to R with the weight on the R/f 'deep'. Push the body round to the R with the L/f behind the R/f. Come up 'high' on L/f. Turn to R with the weight on the R/f. Push the body round to the R with the L/f behind the R/f. Come up 'high' on L/f. Turn to R with the weight on the R/f 'deep'. Push the body round to the R with the L/f behind the R/f. Come up 'high' on L/f. ⎬ Pivot turn to R. This 'pivot turn' is the climax of the refrain and there should be a great release of heartfelt joy as the arms open high and wide above the head and the torso leans into the turn to the right with a gentle rhythm of down/up, down/up, down/up. Let the head also tilt to the right diagonal 'high'.
D	13	1 2 3	*Return to the original quiet mood,* and hands in contact with partners. Step R/f 'high' to R. ⎱ During this movement Bring L/f to R/f — both 'high'. ⎬ the head turns Lower both heels gently to the ground. ⎰ diagonally forward/R.
	14	1 2 3	Step L/f 'high' to L. ⎱ During this movement Bring R/f to L/f — both 'high'. ⎬ the head turns Lower both heels gently to the ground. ⎰ diagonally forward/L.

Music	Bar	Beat	Movement
	15		*Reverence* Keeping the weight of the body on the L/f take the R/f back and come to kneel on the R. At the same time the arms come down to the side and you take the hand of your partners providing a sort of protection for the infant Jesus. The head tilts forward to focus on the infant.
	16		Slowly come up to original *starting position* ready for the second and third verse. *Note:* on the completion of the refrain after the *third verse only*, remain kneeling; in bar 16 the head is quietly lifted and focuses on the cross. The dance finishes in this position.
A	1	1 2 3	**Verse 2** Step R/f 'high' to R. ⎱ During this movement Bring L/f to R/f — both 'high'. ⎰ the head turns Lower both heels gently to the ground. ⎰ diagonally forward/R.
	2	1 2 3	Step L/f 'high' to L. Bring R/f to L/f — both 'high'. Lower both heels gently to the ground. On the second half of the beat bend the knees slightly in preparation for the joyful motif of the next bar.
	3	1	Step forwards 'high' with L/f and bring the R/f to the L on the second half of the beat. At the same time let the arms come up high and wide above the head in praise with palms horizontal and facing upwards. The head is tilted slightly F, with the face forwards 'deep'. Release the hands of your partner.
		2	Stay 'high' and remain still.
		3	Lower both heels gently to the ground. On the second half of the beat bend the knees slightly.
	4	1	Step backwards 'high' with R/f and bring the L/f to the R on the second half of the beat. The arms remain in the position of bar 3. The head is tilted back with the face forward 'high.'
		2	Stay 'high' and remain still.
		3	Lower both heels gently to the ground. On the second half of the beat bend the knees slightly.

Music	Bar	Beat	Movement
B	5	1 2 3	Step L/f 'deep' behind the R/f — to R. Step R/f 'high' to side R. Step L/f 'medium' in front of R/f — to R. On the second half of the beat bend the knee.
	6	1 2 3	Step R/f 'deep' behind the L/f — to L. Step L/f 'high' to side. L. Step R/f 'medium' in front of L/f — to L. On the second half of the beat bend the knees.
	7	1 2 3	Step L/f 'deep' behind R/f to R. Step R/f 'high' forward. Step L/f 'high' forward.
	8	1 2 3	Step R/f 'high' forward. Step L/f 'high' forward. Step R/f 'medium' forward. On the second half of the beat bend the knee slightly. *Note:* release hands for the individual circling. Arms are lowered during the circling. Take the hands of partners again, ready for the Refrain.
C & **D**	9-16		**Refrain, as before.**
A	1	1 2 3	**Verse 3** *Note:* Arms are held low by the side for this verse and not in contact with partners. Step R/f diagonally forward L 'deep' Step L/f forward 'high'. Step R/f forward 'high'.
	2	1 2 3	Step L/f forward 'high'. Step R/f forward 'high'. Lower both heels to the ground. On the second half of the beat bend the R knee and extend the L leg forwards.

(Bars 7–8: A small individual ¾ circular path to the R. Come to face the L ready for Refrain)

(Verse 3, bars 1–2: small individual circle on the spot ... 7/8ths. Focus on the crib.)

Music	Bar	Beat	Movement	
	3	1 2 3	Step L/f diagonally forward R 'high'. Step R/f forward 'high'. Step L/f forward 'high'.	small individual circle on the spot ... 1 1/8th. to come and face centre.
	4	1 2 3	Step R/f forward 'high'. Step L/f forward 'high'. Lower both heels to the ground. On the second half of the beat bend the knees slightly.	
B	5	1 2 3	Step L/f 'deep' behind R/f to R. Step R/f 'high' to R side. Step L/f 'medium' in front of R/f. On the second half of the beat bend the knee slightly.	a gentle rocking effect is sought for here. Remember to focus on the crib at all times.
	6	1 2 3	Step R/f 'deep' behind L/f to L. Step L/f 'high' to side L. Step R/f 'medium' in front of L/f. On the second half of the beat bend the knee slightly.	
	7	1 2 3	Step L/f 'high' behind R/f to R. Step R/f 'high' diagonally forward R Step L/f 'high' forward.	small individual ¾ circle on the spot to the R. Come to face L ready for the last refrain. Take partners' hands.
	8	1 2 3	Step R/f 'high' forward. Step L/f 'high' forward. Step R/f 'medium' forward. On the second half of the beat bend the knee slightly.	
C & D	9-16		**Refrain, as before.** *Note:* on completion of this third repeat of the Refrain, remain kneeling and finish.	

8 Ding Dong Merrily on High

A joyful, uninhibited and energetic nativity dance
based upon the sixteenth century Branle

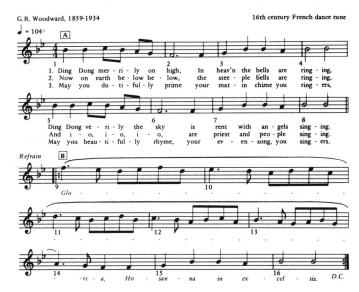

Music	Bar	Beat	Movement
4/4 ♩=104	(circle)		**Starting position** Dancers are spaced alternately men and women, or groups A and B; the man, A, is on the right of the woman, B. Each clasps the hands of the person on either side, arms are held low. All are in position ready to move off to the L, facing the centre of the circle.
A	1	1 2 3 4	Step L/f to L. Hop on L/f. Step R/f behind L. Hop on R/f. ⎱ Travel L
	2	1 2 & 3 4	Step on L/f. Jump from L/f. Land on both feet in place. Wait. ⎰ Travel L
	3	1 2 3 4	Step R/f to R. Hop on R/f. Step L/f behind R. Hop on L/f. ⎱ Travel R
	4	1 2 & 3 4	Step R/f to R. Jump from L/f. Land on both feet in place. Wait. ⎰ Travel R

Music	Bar	Beat	Movement
	5-8		Repeat of bars 1-4.
B	9	1	**Bell ringing motif** Step L/f forward. At the same time the trunk leans forward and arms, which are still in contact with the partner on either side, are flung back behind the body as if pulling the bell rope.
		2	Hop on L/f.
		3	Step R/f back. At the same time the trunk is thrown back and the arms flung forwards.
		4	Hop on R/f.
	10-13		Repeat bar 9, 4 times.
	14	1	Step L/f forward. At the same time the trunk leans forward and arms are flung back behind the body.
		2	Hop on L/f.
		3	Land on both feet in place.
		4	Turn to face partner.
	15-16		During these two bars the man (or A's) takes the woman (or B's) around the waist, lifts her high and places her on his other side. At the same time the woman (or B's) puts her hands on her partners' shoulders and pushes herself high into the air helping her partner achieve the lift.
Repeat B	9-16		The whole bell ringing motif is repeated. The lift in the repeat of the bell ringing motif will of course be with another partner. Your original partner is now on your left. By the end of the dance partners will have been exchanged several times.

Note: Before going back to the beginning for the next verse it is a good idea to have a four bar instrumental interlude. This will give everyone a chance to get their breath back and time to get into a good position to start again.

9 Quem Pastores Laudavere

A quiet, formal nativity dance
based upon the medieval Italian Basse Dance

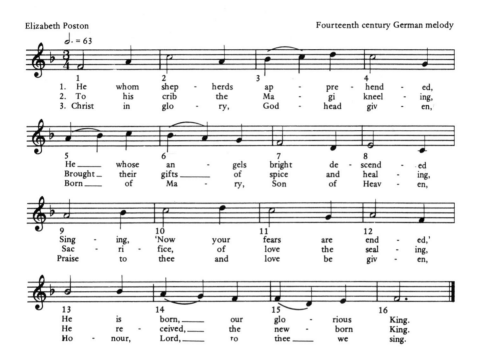

Elizabeth Poston   Fourteenth century German melody

♩. = 63

1. He whom shep - herds ap - pre - hend - ed,
2. To his crib the Ma - gi kneel - ing,
3. Christ in glo - ry, God - head giv - en,

He___ whose an - gels bright de - scend - ed
Brought___ their gifts___ of spice and heal - ing,
Born___ of Ma - ry, Son of Heav - en,

Sing - ing, 'Now your fears are end - ed,'
Sac - ri - fice, of love the seal - ing,
Praise to thee and love be giv - en,

He is born,___ our glo - rious King.
He re - ceived,___ the new - born King.
Ho - nour, Lord,___ to thee___ we sing.

Music	Bar	Beat	Movement
3/4 ♩. = 63	✝		**Starting position** Stand quietly erect with feet together. The head focuses up to the cross. Arms are held loosely at the sides.

Music	Bar	Beat	Movement	
	1	1/2 3	**Motif One** Step L/f forward 'high'. Bring R/f to L/f — both 'high'.	
	2	1/3	Lower both heels slowly to the ground.	
	3	1/2 3	Step R/f forward 'high'. Bring L/f to R/f — both 'high'.	
	4	1/3	Lower both heels slowly to the ground.	Advance forwards with small steps
	5	1/3	Step L/f forward 'high', arms open slightly sideways.	
	6	1/3	Step R/f forward 'high'.	
	7	1/2 3	Step L/f forward 'high'. Bring R/f to L/f — both 'high'.	
	8	1/3	Lower both heels slowly to the ground.	
	9	1/2 3	Step R/f 'high' to R. Bring L/f to R/f — both 'high'.	R
	10	1/3	Lower both heels slowly to the ground.	
	11	1/2 3	Step L/f 'high' to L. Bring R/f to L/f — both 'high'.	L
	12	1/3	Lower both heels slowly to the ground.	
	13/14		Take the R leg back and to the count of 6, i.e. two bars, slowly come to kneel on the right knee. The arms are still held loosely at the sides. During the reverence the head is tilted forward slightly. Keep the back strong and erect.	

Music	Bar	Beat	Movement
	15/16		Bring the weight of the body forward onto the L leg and to the count of 6, i.e. two bars, slowly come to stand as for original position. The arms are held loosely at the side. The head slowly comes up to gaze upon the cross once again. *Note:* all the steps of this dance are very small ones. Long steps will lose something of the quietness and beauty of the dance expression.
			Motif Two: 'Horizontal '8' figure
	1	1/2 3	Step L/f 'high' across R/f. Bring R/f to L/f — both 'high'.
	2	1/3	Lower both heels slowly to the ground.
	3	1/2 3	Step R/f 'high'. Bring L/f to R/f — both 'high'.
	4	1/3	Lower both heels slowly to the ground.
	5	1/3	Step L/f forward 'high'.
	6	1/3	Step R/f forward 'high'.
	7	1/2 3	Step L/f forward 'high'. Bring R/f to L/f — both 'high'.
	8	1/3	Lower both heels slowly to the ground. *Note:* During this first set of eight bars each dancer completes a small 7/8 circular pathway coming to face slightly diagonally/forward L on bar 8 i.e. Throughout the motif keep the head focused high to the cross.

Small circle R.

— 39 —

Music	Bar	Beat	Movement
	9	1/2 3	Step R/f forward 'high' across L/f. Bring L/f to R/f — both 'high'.
	10	1/3	Lower both heels slowly to the ground.
	11	1/2 3	Step L/f forward 'high'. Bring R/f to L/f — both 'high'.
	12	1/3	Lower both heels slowly to the ground.
	13	1/3	Step R/f forward 'high'.
	14	1/3	Step L/f forward 'high'.
	15	1/2 3	Step R/f forward 'high'. Bring L/f to R/f — both 'high.'
	16	1/3	Lower both heels slowly to the ground.

Note: During this second set of eight bars each dancer completes an individual 7/8 circular pathway which should bring them back to face the cross.

Small circle L.

Motif Three: Figure 'S'

Music	Bar	Beat	Movement
	1	1/2 3	Step R/f diagonally forward 'high'. Step L/f forward 'deep'.
	2	1/2 3	Step R/f forward 'high'. Step L/f forward 'deep'.
	3	1/2 3	Step R/f forward 'high'. Step L/f forward 'deep'.
	4	1 2 3	Step R/f forward 'high'. Step L/f forward 'high'. Step R/f forward 'deep'.

½ circle to R.

Music	Bar	Beat	Movement	
	5	1/2 3	Step L/f diagonally forward 'high'. Step R/f forward 'deep'.	
	6	1/2 3	Step L/f forward 'high'. Step R/f forward 'deep'.	½ circle to L. Continue circle to face front.
	7	1/2 3	Step L/f forward 'high'. Step R/f forward 'deep'.	
	8	1 2 3	Step L/f forward 'high'. Step R/f forward 'high'. Step L/f forward 'deep'.	
			Reverence and Conclusion	
	9	1/2 3	Step R/f to R 'high'. Turn body to diag. R. Bring L/f to R — both 'high'.	
	10	1/3	Lower both heels slowly to the ground.	
	11	1/2 3	Step L/f to L 'high'. Turn body to diag. L. Bring R/f to L — both 'high'.	
	12	1/3	Lower both heels slowly to the ground.	
	13/14		Take the R leg back and to the count of 6, i.e. two bars, slowly come to kneel on R knee. The arms are still held loosely to the sides. During the reverence the head is tilted forward slightly. Keep the back strong and erect.	
	15/16		Retain the kneeling position, and for the last two bars slowly bring the head up and focus on the cross.	

Note: Fundamental to this dance is the geometry implicit in the floor patterns. Considerable care needs to be taken with this. Make sure that the dancers start with an equal distance between them, and that this spacing is retained throughout.

Another point to note is that throughout the dance the eye focuses always on the cross.

I have placed the dance for five dancers, but of course any number may be used. I hasten to add, however, that problems with regard to spacing are greatly increased by larger numbers.

10 Adoramus te Domine

WE ADORE YOU, O LORD

A quiet, sensitive meditative dance
based upon a very simple vocabulary,
and ideal for both large and small numbers

Music © 1978, 1980, 1981 Les Presses de Taizé (France)

Music	Bar	Beat	Movement
4/4 ♩=80		↑	**Starting position** The dancers 'place' themselves within the four part canon groups indicated in the diagram. All stand tall with feet together, arms held by the side. The head is tilted slightly forward.
	1 & 2		**Motif 1A** Let the arms 'breathe' away slightly from the sides of the body before bringing them across the body R over L going across, out and up, open wide and high above the head with the palms facing upwards. At the same time the face comes to focus forward 'high' on the cross. This motif is performed in a four part canon, each group coming in one after the other at the appropriate beat.
	3 & 4		**Motif 1B** ALL the groups slowly bring the arms down in unison, moving outwards and down to the side to the count of two bars i.e. 8 beats. The head is tilted forward once again. The dance consists of 17 'statements' of the music, beginning with two instrumental statements.

Music	Bar	Beat	Movement
1st Statement	1-4		Instrumental Introduction.
2nd Statement	1-4		Instrumental Introduction. The instrumental introduction has a two-fold function: firstly it helps evoke an appropriate spiritual atmosphere and secondly it gives the dancers time to get into 'place'.
3rd Statement	1	1-2 3-4	Group A Group B } Each group in turn performs *Motif 1A*, taking two beats to do so. Each group holds the final position of this Motif until group D has completed it.
	2	1-2 3-4	Group C Group D } This will mean that the first group will remain holding the first movement longer than the second and third. The fourth group will not have time to hold the movement position at all.
	3-4	1-8	All groups perform MOTIF 1B. Make sure that the full eight beats are used for the movement.
4th Statement	1-4		Repeat of statement 3.
5th Statement	1-4		Stand still, in quiet contemplation, with the eyes focussed on the cross forward 'high'.
6th Statement	1	1-2 3-4	Group D Group C } Each group in turn performs *Motif 1A*, taking two beats to do so. Each group holds the final position of this Motif until group A has completed it.
	2	1-2 3-4	Group B Group A }
	3-4		All groups perform *Motif 1B*.
7th Statement	1-4		Repeat of 6th Statement.
8th Statement	1-4		Stand still, in quiet contemplation, with the eyes focussed on the cross forward 'high'.

Music	Bar	Beat	Movement
9th Statement	1	1-2 3-4	Group A Group B } All in turn perform Motif 1A.
	2	1-2 3-4	Group C Group D
	3-4	1-8	All groups perform MOTIF 1B. *Note:* As the arms come down to the side, take the R leg back and come to kneel on the R knee. The head is tilted forward slightly. Be ready to come up on the L leg for the next statement.
10th Statement	1	1-2 3-4	Group A Group B } All in turn perform MOTIF 1A.
	2	1-2 3-4	Group C Group D } *Note:* Step up boldly on the L leg from the kneeling position into the motif.
	3-4	1-8	All groups perform MOTIF 1B, but as with the previous development of this motif, come to kneel on the R knee by stepping back with the R leg.
11th Statement	1-4		Kneel still, in quiet contemplation, with the eyes focussed on the cross forward 'high'.
12th Statement	1	1-2 3-4	Group D Group C } All in turn perform MOTIF 1A.
	2	1-2 3-4	Group B Group A } *Note:* Step up boldly on the L leg from the kneeling position into the motif.
	3-4	1-8	All groups perform *Motif 1B*. *Note:* Come to kneel on R knee by taking the R leg back.
13th Statement	1-4		Repeat of 12th Statement *Note:* Do *not* kneel. Remain standing facing the cross.

Music	Bar	Beat	Movement
14th Statement	1-4		Stand still, in quiet contemplation, with the eyes focussed on the cross forward 'high'.
15th Statement	1-4		**New Motif** Whilst standing relaxed and tall, slowly turn the head to the R so that it looks over the shoulder. Leading with the R shoulder turn the body on the spot to the R. Let the head and shoulder lead you round until you come to face the altar again. This takes up the full 4 bars.
16th Statement	1-2	1-8	With the head upturned, bring the arms out away from the body, and gradually wide and high above the head.
	3-4	1-8	Hold the above position.
17th Statement	1-2	1-8	Slowly let the arms come down to the side.
	3-4	1-8	Taking the R leg back, come to kneel on the R knee. The head focuses on the cross.

DANCE 'PLACING'

The actual positioning of the dance and dancers is as important as dance steps. Frequently this aspect of choreography is neglected or underestimated. The careful placing of the dancers both as individuals and as a group is an important and fundamental consideration. Recognizing also that buildings have an important influence on the placing of the dance I suggest some possible ideas.

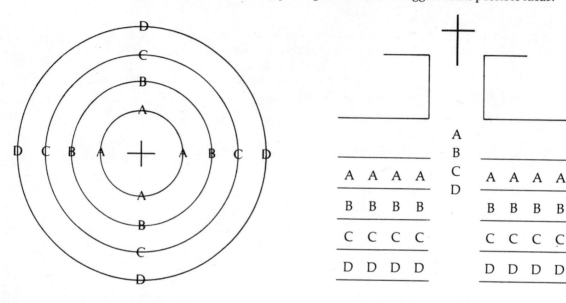

(a) *A setting that has the cross at the centre and which allows worshippers to surround the altar.*

(b) *The traditional church setting. Sometimes there is space in the chancel for the formation of (a) and (c).*

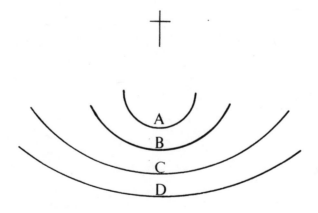

(c) *A semi-circular setting.*

Note: for other ideas about 'placing' see 'Salvator Mundi', Dance No.3 above.

MUSICAL ACCOMPANIMENT

What I have to say here about the relationship between music and Adoramus te Domine is applicable to music in general, and to the music of Taizé in particular.

One of the problems for the Director of Music in these simple Taizé pieces is that of keeping the repetition fresh and alive through careful and sensitive use of musical colour — both instrumental and vocal.

The seventeen 'statements' in the choreography correspond to the seventeen statements in the recording made by Taizé. This will be helpful to dance groups who do not have a choir or who would rather have the arrangement from Taizé. But there will be many groups who would hope to have a live accompaniment. The musical arrangements that I suggest here are designed to fit the character of the choreography. If the Musical Director could, initially at least, adhere to this plan it would help the dance. In the meditative sections of statements 5, 8, 11, and 14, where the dancers are still, there is a particular need for musical/spiritual sensitivity and this will provide a good opportunity for the musicians to be individually creative.

For a detailed discussion about ideas of orchestration and musical development generally see *Music from Taizé* (Collins, 1982), pp.20ff.

Suggested musical structure for Adoramus te Domine

1st/2nd Statement	Quiet instrumental introduction during which the spiritual/dramatic mood is set and the dancers move into their positions.
3rd Statement 4th Statement 5th Statement	Full Choir. Solo Choral Group. Meditative interlude — choral backdrop with solo obligato (instrumental).
6th Statement 7th Statement 8th Statement	Solo Choral Group. Full Choir. Meditative interlude — choral backdrop with solo obligato (instrumental).
9th Statement 10th Statement 11th Statement	Full Choir. Solo Choral Group. Meditative Interlude — choral backdrop with solo obligato (instrumental).
12th Statement 13th Statement 14th Statement	Solo Group. Full Choir. Meditative Interlude — choral backdrop with solo obligato (instrumental).
15th Statement 16th Statement 17th Statement	For the next three statements there is a need for different colouring. The dance is being brought to a close now and this feeling should be reflected in the music. This needs to be negotiated with the dancers.

11 Gloria

GLORY TO GOD IN THE HIGHEST! ALLELUIA!

A four part movement canon

This interpretation of the Gloria belongs more to heaven than to earth. It is not exuberant. Rather, it is slow and dignified, based upon a recognition of the unchanging, the mysterious and the wondrous.

Music	Bar	Beat	Movement
6/8 ♩=76			**Starting position** This is a very simple dance for a large number of people. Dancers form four circles. The space between each circle and between each dancer needs to be carefully worked out. Each dancer clasps the hand of the person on both R and L. Arms are held low. All face the centre of the circle ready to move off to the L facing L.

Music	Bar	Beat	Movement
A	1	1 2	Step L/f forward. Step R/f forward. ⎞
	2	2 2	Step L/f forward. Step R/f forward. ⎟ Travel clockwise and face that direction.
B	3	1 2	Step L/f forward. Step R/f forward. ⎟
	4	1 & 2	Step L/f forward. ⎠ On the second half of the beat turn to the R. Bring R/f to L but keep body weight on L/f. During these seven steps the arms are slowly and confidently brought up high and wide above the head, still clasping the hands of the person on either side, the L arm coming to the front and the R arm coming to the back.
C	5	1 2	Step R/f forward. Step L/f forward. ⎞
	6	1 2	Step R/f forward. Step L/f forward. ⎠ Travel anticlockwise and face that direction. Bring the arms down in bar 5.
D	7/8		Pivot turn on the R/f to the R. Release hands for turn. Finish turn on R/f, ready to start bar 1 again on the L/f. Take partners' hands again. Return to A.

Gloria may be danced in unison, either in one circle or more but it is most effective when danced in 4 circles as a four part movement canon. As with a musical canon each group, starting with group A in the centre, takes the theme at the appropriate time as marked in the music A B C & D

Ideally all the dancers sing as well as move.

There is a considerable amount of coming and going and with four groups dancing in canon great care needs to be taken in realising these simple motifs, otherwise the whole becomes a mess. Spacing between the four groups and spacing between individuals is particularly important. Make sure also that the movements are performed exactly in time together. Although the dance moves from left to right again and again, there is a general movement all the time towards the LEFT. To finish the dance simply come to stand still and quiet after the 'pivot turn'.

12 Dance Project — Psalm 95

Now that we have worked on a variety of choreographic/scriptural ideas and have learnt a variety of dances let us see how we might apply some of this material in working on a dance interpretation of Psalm 95.

The interpretation I propose is not to give a literal or mimetic translation of the text, but rather to express an inner, heartfelt meaning and response to the text, that aspect of meaning which cannot be understood or expressed in words. Through the impressions and expressions of this dance something of the ineffable, the mystical content of this Psalm will be our concern. It is the understanding of the heart rather than mind or words and propositions. Whilst our study will be rooted in scripture and will certainly involve a study of the text, the expression and understanding in the dance is in a sense something separate from and more than the text.

I have taken the New International Version* of the Psalm.

1. Come, let us sing for joy to the Lord;
   let us shout aloud to the Rock of our salvation.
   Let us come before him with thanksgiving
   and extol him with music and song.

2. For the Lord is the great God,
   the great King above all gods.
   In his hand are the depths of the earth,
   and the mountain peaks belong to him.
   The sea is his, for he made it,
   and his hands formed the dry land.

   Come, let us bow down in worship,
   let us kneel before the Lord our Maker;
   for he is our God
   and we are the people of his pasture,
   the flock under his care.

3. Today, if you hear his voice,
   do not harden your hearts as you did as Meribah,
   as you did that day at Massah in the desert,
   where your fathers tested and tried me,
   though they had seen what I did.
   For forty years I was angry with that generation;
   I said, "They are a people whose hearts go astray,
   and they have not known my ways."
   So I declared an oath in my anger,
   "They shall never enter my rest."

It will be seen that the Psalm is divided into several dramatically distinct sections:

Section One	Invitation
Section Two	Adoration
Section Three	Admonition
Section Four	Affirmation

*Copyright © 1978 by New York International Bible Society.

Section One: Invitation

The opening of the psalm is an invitation to come and sing praises unto his name, to shout aloud, to come before him with thanksgiving and extol him with music and song.

This invitation could be given by the minister or one of the dance leaders; the fellowship responds by coming out of their seats into an appropriate dance space to dance the extended version of *In the presence of your people*, (dance no.4 above).

Section Two: Adoration

On the completion of the invitation, the dancers perhaps sit where they are and present the second section in the following way.
1st voice
    The Lord is a great God.
2nd voice
    Yes, a great king above all Gods.
3rd voice
    In his hands are all the corners of the earth.
4th voice
    The mountain peaks are his also.
5th voice
    The sea is his, for he made it.
6th voice
    His hands prepared the dry land.
All (speaking in a hushed voice with a sense of awe and wonder)
    Come, let us bow down in worship
    Let us kneel before the Lord our maker,
    For he is our God and we are the people of his pasture
    And the flock under his care.

Starting from an informal sitting or kneeling position, I suggest that this call to prayer and adoration is expressed through the dance *Adoramus te Domine* (dance no.10 above).

Section Three: Admonition

    Today, if you hear his voice,
    do not harden your hearts as you did at Meriba,
    as you did at Massah in the desert,
    where your fathers tested and tried me
    though they had seen what I did.
    For forty years I was angry with that generation;
    I said, "They are a people whose hearts go astray,
    and they have not known my ways."
    So I declared an oath in my anger,
    "They shall not enter my rest."

This admonition might be read by the leader of the congregation.

Section Four: Affirmation

We affirm our faith through the dance *Father we adore you* (dance no.1 above).

Conclusion

Finish with the dance you began with *In the presence of your people*, or possibly *God has spoken* (dance no.6 above).

Conclusion

These dances are not simply concerned with the literal and mimetic translation of the words of the text, nor with the development of a movement vocabulary for its own sake. Nor is their chief concern the aesthetic and beauty of movement, pattern, shape and design, or physical skill and spectacle. Rather it is with 'saying' what words can never 'say'.

Dance 'is a way of expressing the spiritual animation that swells from the depths of the human heart' (Brother Robert of Taizé) — that which is beyond words. All too often our worship is dominated by the word to the exclusion of other 'languages', other ways of knowing and understanding. The language of words is but one of many languages through which we can come to know and express ourselves. Above all the non-verbal languages of music and dance are peculiarly 'languages' of the heart and the heart is essential to true worship. Of course the heart can be related to words but there is an expression of the heart unique to dance and music, separate from and beyond words. Accordingly the focus of these dances is with the evocation and articulation of the ineffable, spiritual, inner and heartfelt knowledge and understanding of our faith and worship. Whilst the literal text, the mimetic and aesthetic are important considerations, and in the case of the word fundamental, they are secondary in the dances.

'It is with the heart that you are justified, and it is with your mouth that you confess and are saved.' *Romans 10:10.*

'God is spirit and his worshippers must worship in spirit and in truth.' *John 4:24.*

'These people come near to me with their mouths and honour me with their lips but their hearts are far from me.' *Isaiah 29:13; Matthew 15:8.*

As David Watson says in *I Believe in Evangelism* ... 'This is not spiritual experience separate from the word. The spirit is bound to the word. The church which abandons the link with the word and tries to rely on the spirit falls prey to all the evils of spiritual enthusiasms. Conversely a church which tries to rely only on the word and tries to reduce the spirit to the word, falls prey to all the evils of verbalistic enthusiasm'. (Hodder and Stoughton, 1976).

'When the bible speaks of the heart, it does not mean the physical organs which pump blood around the body, but rather the centre of man's emotions, desires, affections. With the mind we become informed; with the heart we become involved.' (J. Blanchard, *Right With God*, Banner of Faith Trust).

P. H. Phenix in *Realms of Meaning* (McGraw-Hill, 1964) describes how some 'languages' are bridges to our knowing and understanding whilst other languages are barriers to our knowing and understanding; some are appropriate and some are inappropriate. Propositional knowledge as expressed in words is not always appropriate to all situations in our life:

'Revelation does not mean a mere passing over into the intelligible and comprehensible. Something may be profoundly and intimately known in feeling for the bliss it brings and the agitation it produces, and yet the understanding may find no concept for it. To know and to understand conceptually are two different things and often even mutually exclusive and contrasted'. (Otto, *The Idea of the Holy*, Oxford, 1923).

'Vocabularies are formed by the mind over long periods and are capable of expressing whatever the mind is capable of entertaining. But when the heart on its knees, moves in the awesome presence and hears with fear and wonder things not lawful to utter, then the mind falls flat. There is a difference between theological knowledge and spiritual experience, the difference between knowing God by hearsay and knowing him by acquaintance ... and the difference is not merely verbal; it is real and serious and vital'. (A. W. Tozer, *Born After Midnight*, Christian Pub. Inc.).

There are many ways through which one can come to know and understand the Christian faith and the language of words is but one way of articulating and making sense of our world. Dance constitutes one of these ways, a legitimate non-verbal expression. So, 'Come, let us praise his name in the dance'.

Dances Expressed in Labanotation

1 Father We Adore You

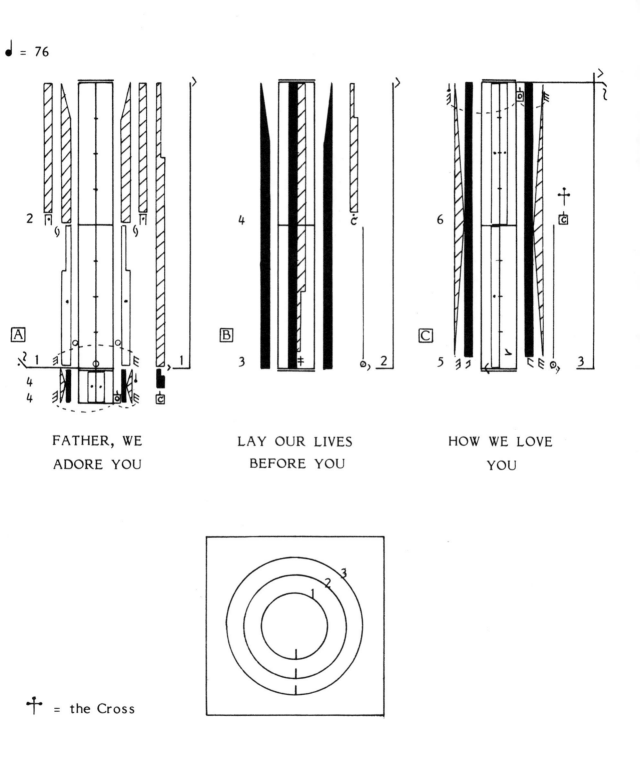

FATHER, WE
ADORE YOU

LAY OUR LIVES
BEFORE YOU

HOW WE LOVE
YOU

✝ = the Cross

2 Sing to our Father

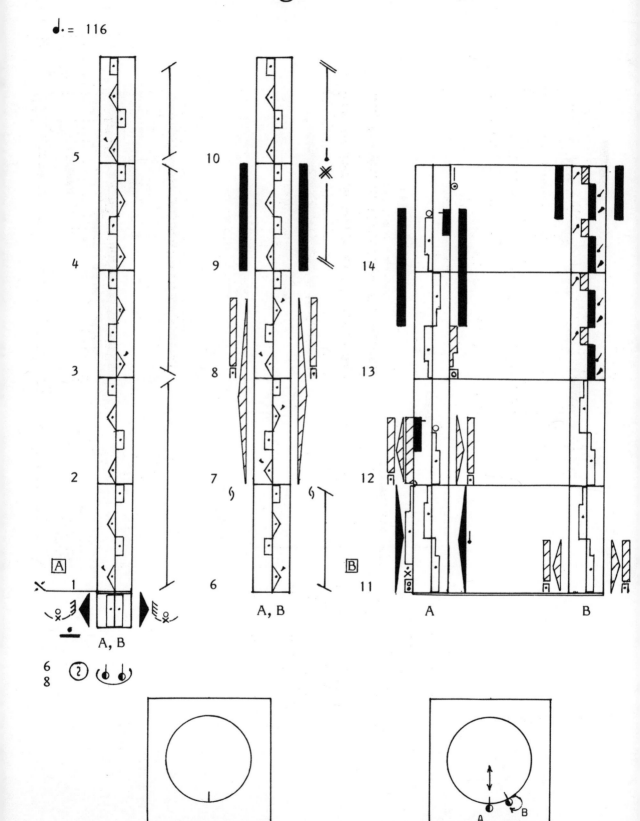

Sing to our Father — continued

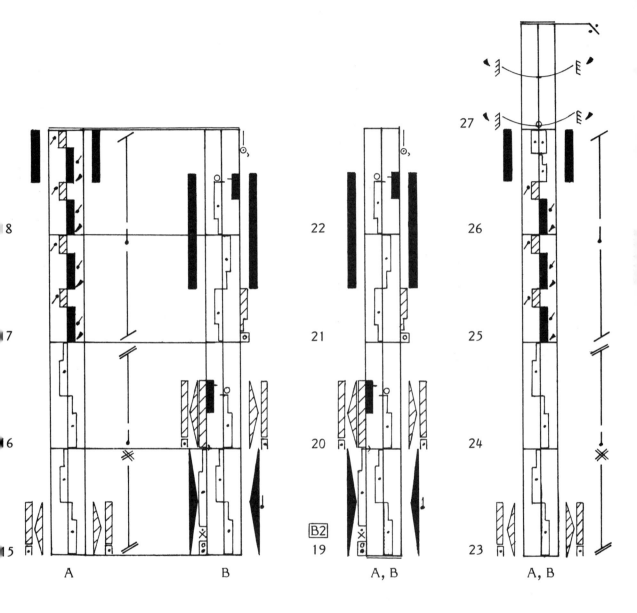

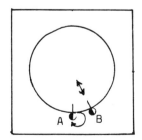

3 Salvator Mundi

♩ = 80

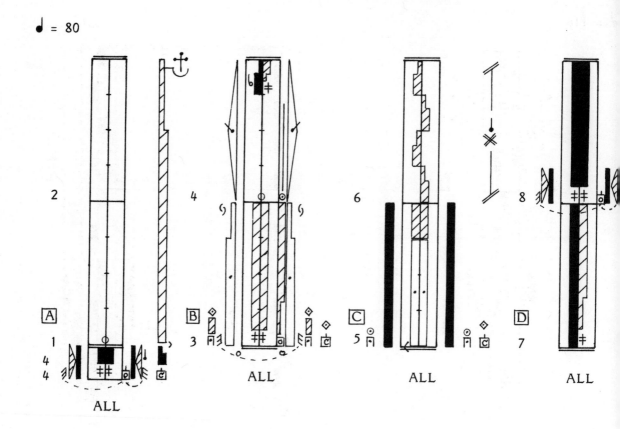

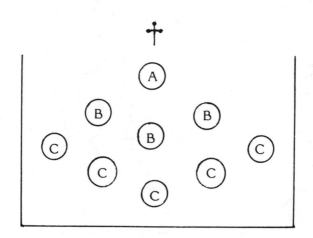

See word notes for other possible group formations
and possibilities for canon form.

4 In the Presence of Your People

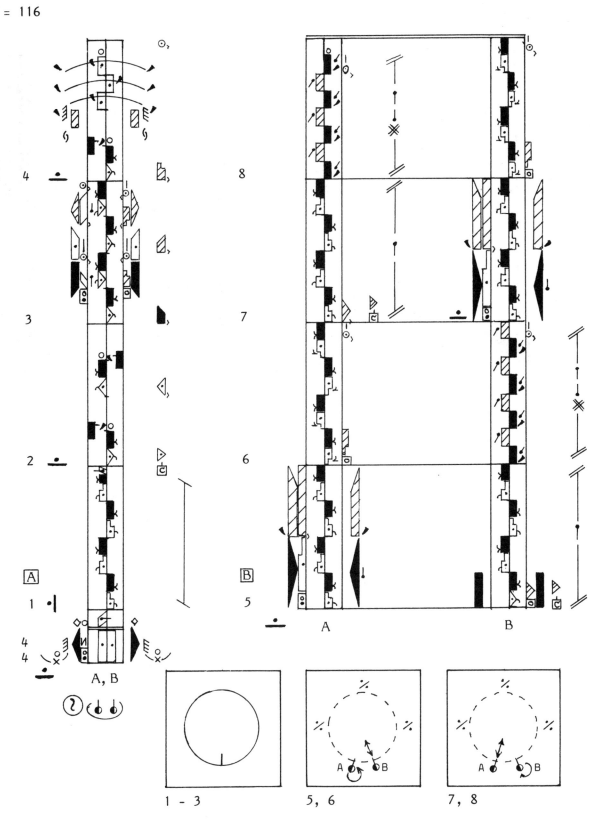

5 Prayer of St Francis

♩ = 84

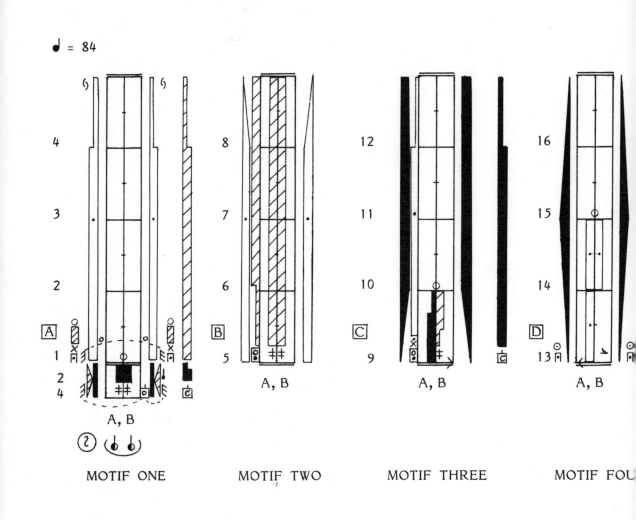

MOTIF ONE   MOTIF TWO   MOTIF THREE   MOTIF FOU[R]

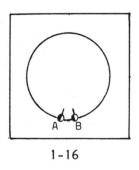

1-16

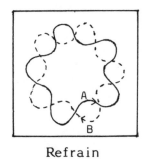

Refrain

Note: MOTIF FOUR
is followed by the
Refrain, the 'peace'
in the form of a
'hey'.

6 God Has Spoken

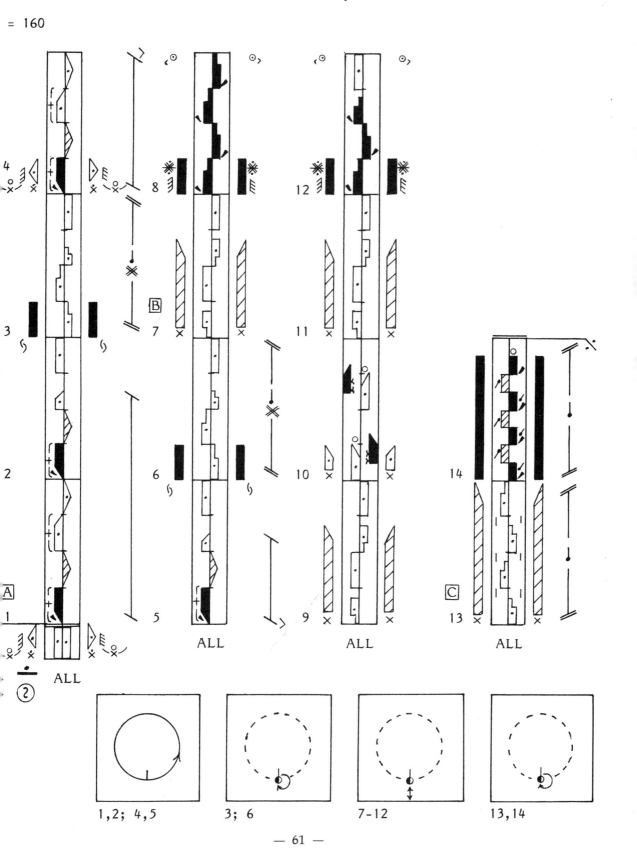

7 Infant Holy, Infant Lowly

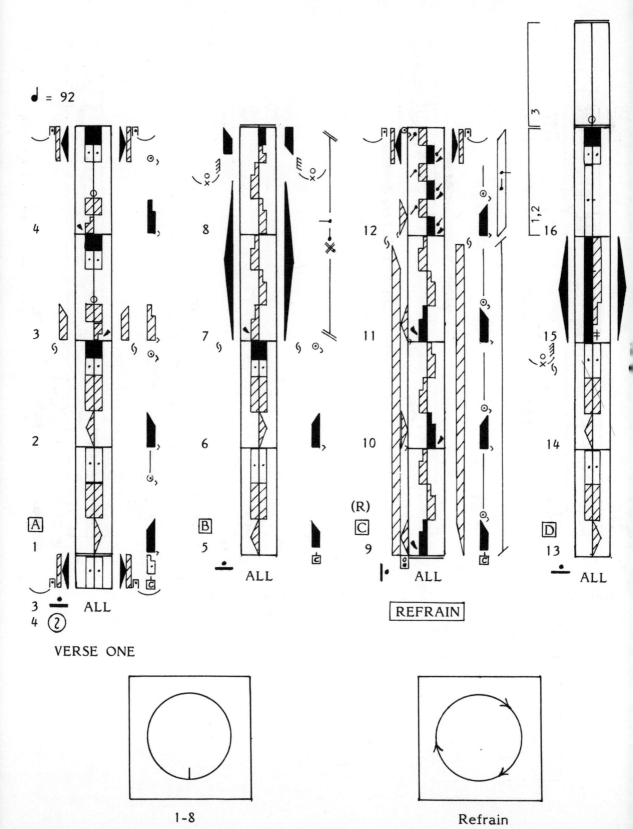

VERSE ONE

REFRAIN

1-8

Refrain

Infant Holy, Infant Lowly — continued

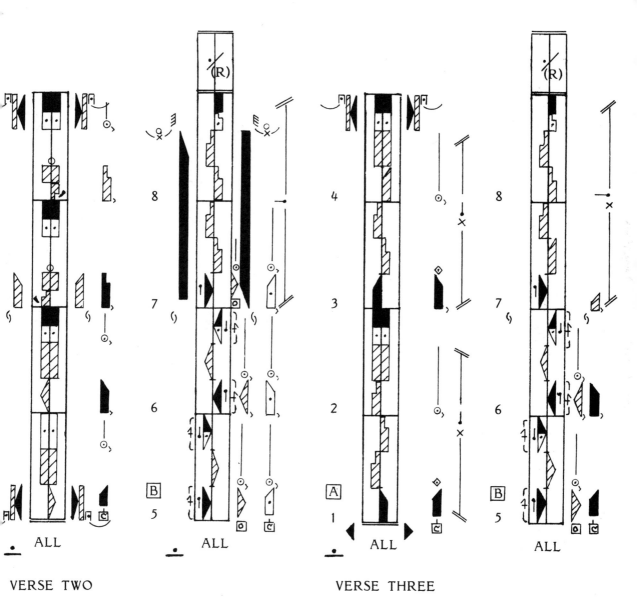

VERSE TWO

VERSE THREE

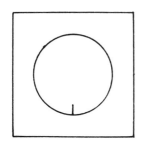

(R) = Refrain

8 Ding Dong Merrily on High

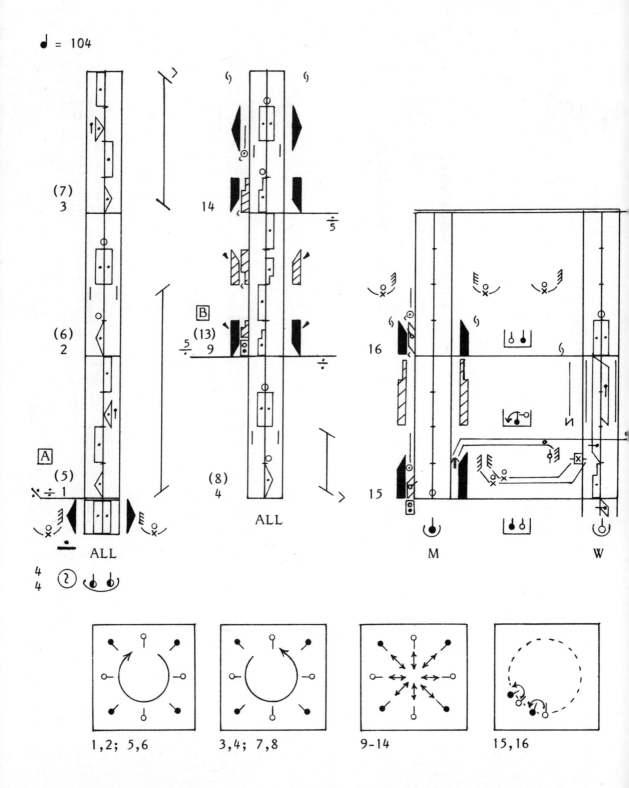

9 Quem Pastores Laudavere

MOTIF ONE

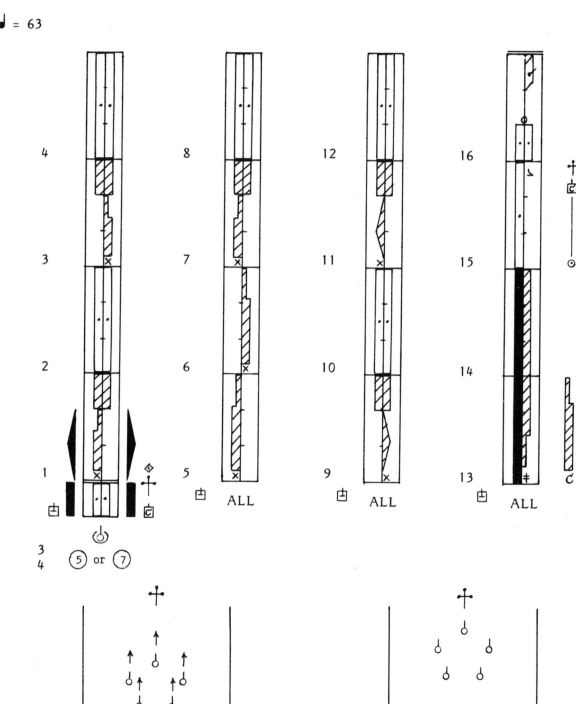

Quem Pastores Laudavere — continued

MOTIF TWO

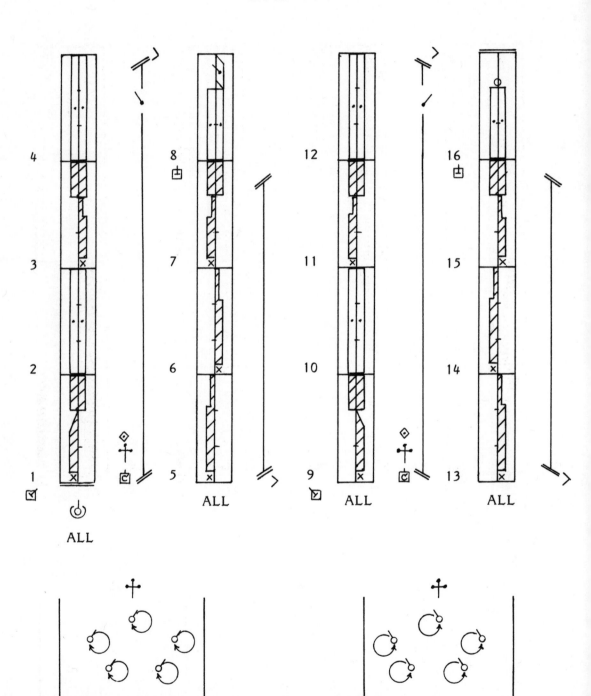

ALL

1-8

9-16

MOTIF THREE

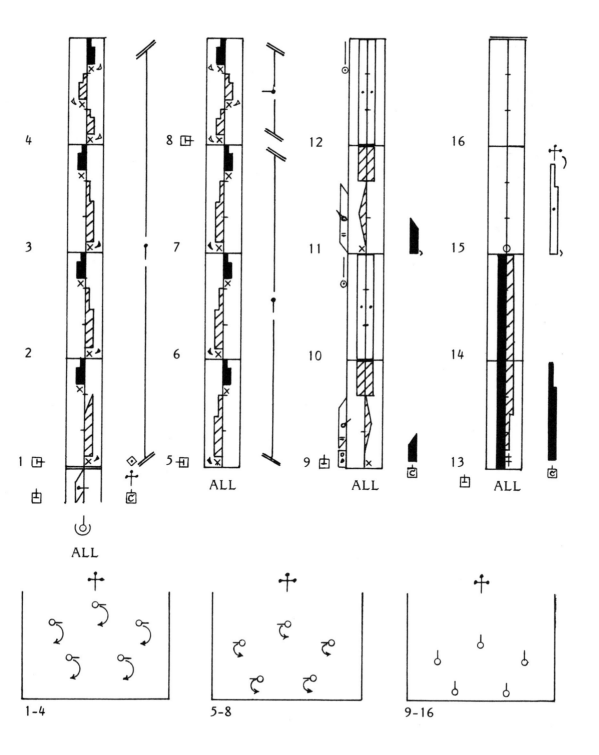

10 Adoramus te Domine

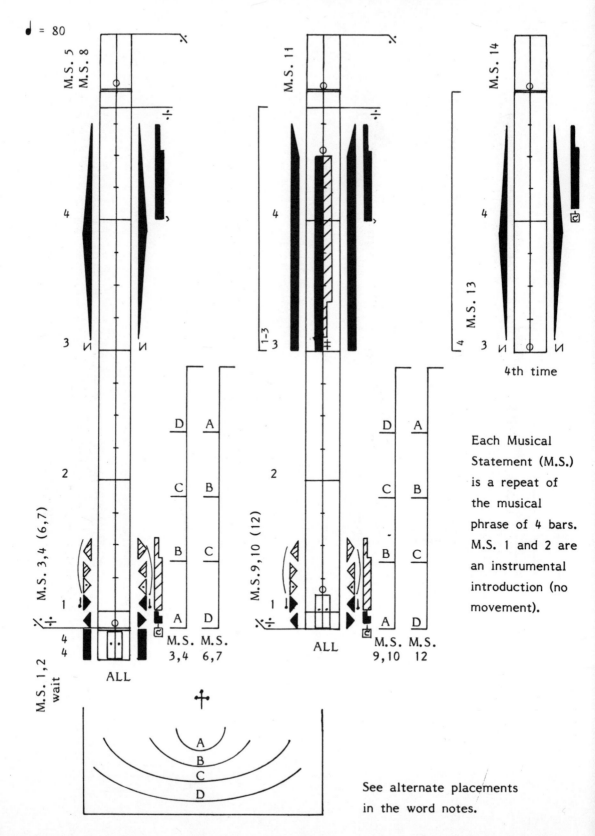

Each Musical
Statement (M.S.)
is a repeat of
the musical
phrase of 4 bars.
M.S. 1 and 2 are
an instrumental
introduction (no
movement).

See alternate placements
in the word notes.

Adoramus te Domine — continued

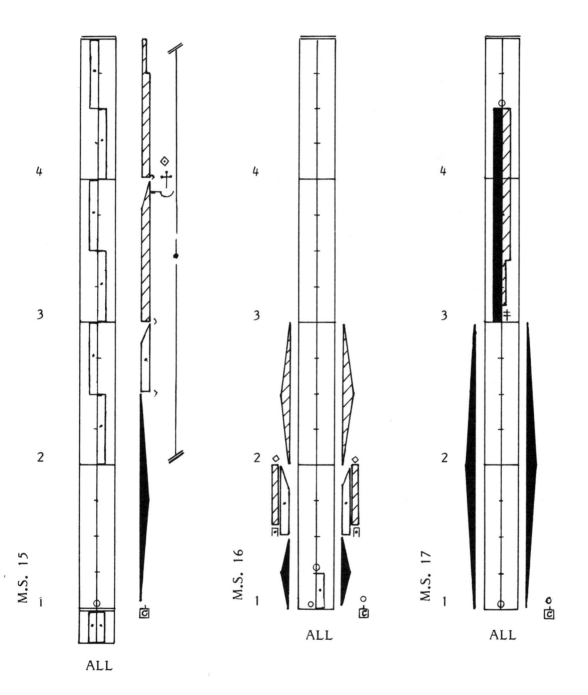

11 Gloria

$\bullet$ = 76

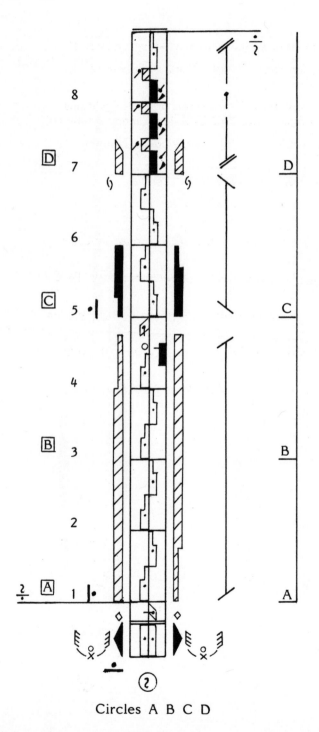

Circles A B C D

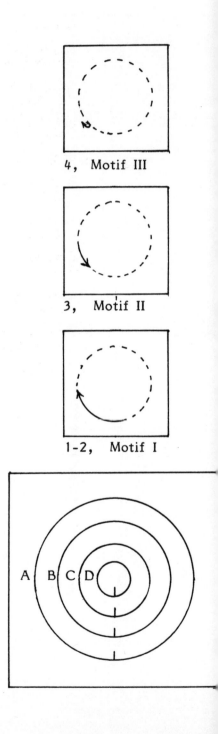

4, Motif III

3, Motif II

1-2, Motif I

Sources of Printed Music and Recordings

1 Father we adore you: *Sound of Living Waters*, Hodder, London.

2 Sing to our Father: *Cry, Hosanna*, Hodder, London. Fisherfolk Recordings.

3 Salvator Mundi: *Music from Taizé* (instrumental and vocal editions) Collins, London. Recording: Taizé 3005 TZ2040, 'Canons et Litanies'.

4 In the presence of your people: *Cry, Hosanna*, Hodder, London. Fisherfolk Recordings.

5 Make me an instrument: *Fresh Sounds*, Hodder, London.

6 God has spoken: *Sound of Living Waters*, Hodder, London. Record: SPA 501.

7 Infant holy, infant lowly: *Kingsway Carol Book*, compiled by Leslie Russell.

8 Ding dong merrily on high: *Penguin Book of Christmas Carols*, Penguin, London.

9 Quem Pastors Laudavere: *Penguin Book of Christmas Carols*, Penguin, London.

10 Adoremus te Domine: *Music from Taizé*, Collins, London. Recording: Taizé 3003, 'Notre Dame de Paris'.

11 Gloria: *Music from Taizé*, Collins, London. Taizé 3005, Cantate.

Further Reading

PRACTICAL DANCE BOOKS

Priscilla and Robert Lobley: *Your book of English country dancing*, Faber & Faber, London, 1980.

Cecil Sharp: *Country dance books.* (Many editions, all out of print, but available from libraries.)

Joan Lawson: *European folk dance*, Imperial Society of Teachers of Dancing, London.

Melusine Wood: *Historical dances*, Dance Books, London, 1982.

Mable Dolmetsch: *Dances of England and France, 1450-1600*, Da Capo, New York, 1976.

Mable Dolmetsch: *Dances of Spain and Italy, 1400-1600*, Da Capo, New York, 1975.

Ann Hutchinson: *Your move*, Gordon and Breach, London, 1983.

NOTATION BOOKS

Ann Hutchinson: *Labanotation*, Theatre Arts, New York, 1977.

Ann Kipling Brown and Monica Parker: *Dance notation for beginners — Benesh movement notation and Labanotation*, Dance Books, London, 1983.

THEORETICAL BOOKS ON DANCE COMPOSITION

Lois Ellfeldt: *A primer for choreographers*, Dance Books, London, 1974.

Doris Humphrey: *The art of making dances*, Dance Books, London, 1976.

Valerie Preston-Dunlop: *A handbook for dance in education*, Macdonald & Evans, Plymouth, 1984.

Betty Redfearn: *Concepts in modern educational dance*, Dance Books, London, 1982.

Jacqueline M. Smith: *Dance composition, a practical guide for teachers*, Lepus Books, London, 1976.

THEOLOGICAL DISCUSSION OF DANCE IN WORSHIP

J. B. Gross: *The parson on dancing*, Dance Horizons, New York, 1975.

William O. E. Oesterley: *The sacred dance*, (Several editions, all out of print, but available from libraries).

The books on this list, and many others on dance, may be obtained from: Dance Books Ltd., 9 Cecil Court, St Martin's Lane, London WC2N 4EZ.